FROM DARKNESS TO LIGHT

A Theological Journey

Dr. Maxwell Shimba

TABLE OF CONTENTS

PREFACE

In every human heart lies an innate longing for light, a yearning to escape the shadows of sin, suffering, and despair. This longing finds its ultimate fulfillment in the transformative journey from darkness to light, a journey that is central to the Christian faith. "Darkness to Light: A Theological Journey" seeks to explore this profound transformation through the lens of Scripture, offering insights and reflections that illuminate the path toward spiritual enlightenment and eternal hope.

The concept of moving from darkness to light is woven throughout the Bible, from the creation narrative in Genesis, where God speaks light into existence, to the apocalyptic visions in Revelation, where the glory of God provides eternal illumination. This journey is not merely an abstract theological construct but a lived experience, marked by struggles, redemption, faith, forgiveness, holiness, and ultimately, the eternal light of God's presence.

Each chapter of this book delves into different facets of this journey. We begin by examining the human condition, recognizing the pervasive brokenness that sin has wrought in our lives and the world. From there, we explore the promise of redemption offered through Jesus Christ, the journey of faith that requires trust and surrender, and the transformative power of forgiveness.

As we progress, we consider what it means to walk in the light, the importance of overcoming trials, and the hope of resurrection that assures us of life beyond the grave. We then reflect on the boundless grace of God, the call to holiness that beckons us to reflect His character, and the ultimate culmination of our journey in the eternal light of His presence.

The purpose of this book is not only to provide theological insights but also to offer practical guidance for living a life that moves steadily from darkness to light. It is my hope that readers will find encouragement, inspiration, and a renewed sense of purpose as they engage with the biblical truths presented here.

To those embarking on this journey, whether you are a seasoned believer or someone seeking answers to life's deepest questions, know that the path from darkness to light is one of profound transformation and divine promise. As you read these pages, may you encounter the God who calls you out of darkness into His marvelous light and experience the joy and peace that come from walking in His presence.

May the light of Christ shine brightly in your hearts and guide you ever closer to the eternal glory that awaits you. In His Name,

Dr. Maxwell Shimba

ix

DR. MAXWELL SHIMBA

INTRODUCTION

The journey from darkness to light is a profound and transformative experience that touches the core of our existence. It is a journey that transcends mere intellectual assent or emotional response; it is a journey that encompasses the entirety of our being. In this book, "From Darkness to Light: A Theological Journey," we will explore the depths of this transformation through the lens of Scripture, seeking to understand the profound truths that guide us from the shadows of sin and despair into the radiant light of God's love and grace.

The concept of darkness is not foreign to us. It is a metaphor that permeates our lives, symbolizing confusion, fear, ignorance, and sin. We live in a world where darkness often seems to dominate, where brokenness and suffering are all too common. The Bible speaks of this darkness in stark terms, illustrating the dire condition of humanity apart from God. In the opening chapter of Genesis, we see the earth described as "formless and empty, darkness was over the surface of the deep" (Genesis 1:2). This depiction of chaos and void sets the stage for the dramatic intervention of God, who speaks light into existence, bringing order and life.

Just as the physical world was plunged into darkness and brought into light through God's creative word, so too are our lives transformed by His redemptive power. The darkness of sin, which entered the world through Adam and Eve's disobedience, has cast a long shadow over humanity. It has alienated us from God, disrupted our relationships with one another, and marred the image of God within us. Yet, amidst this bleak reality, the Bible offers a message of hope and restoration.

At the heart of this message is the person of Jesus Christ. He is the light of the world, sent by the Father to dispel the darkness and bring us into the glorious light of His presence. The Gospel of John proclaims, "In him was life, and that life was the light of all mankind. The light shines in the darkness, and the darkness has not overcome it" (John 1:4-5). This powerful declaration sets the tone for our exploration, as we seek to understand the implications of Christ's light in our lives.

Throughout this book, we will journey through ten chapters that each address a critical aspect of moving from darkness to light. We will begin by examining the human condition, acknowledging the reality of sin and our need for redemption. From there, we will explore the promise of salvation offered through Jesus Christ and the journey of faith that ensues. We will delve into the transformative power of forgiveness, the importance of walking in the light, and the hope found in the resurrection.

We will also address the challenges we face, such as overcoming trials and embracing grace. These chapters will provide practical insights and biblical wisdom to help us navigate the complexities of life while keeping our eyes fixed on the eternal light of God. Finally, we will conclude with a look at the call to holiness and the ultimate destination of our journey – the eternal presence of God, where His glory will be our everlasting light.

This book is not merely an academic exercise; it is an invitation to experience the life-changing power of God's Word. As we embark on this theological journey together, my prayer is that you will be encouraged, challenged, and inspired to move from darkness to light. May you come to know the depth of God's love, the power of His grace, and the hope of His promises. And may you walk confidently in the light of His truth, knowing that the darkness can never overcome it.

Let us begin this journey with hearts open to the leading of the Holy Spirit, minds receptive to the truth of Scripture, and lives ready to be transformed by the light of Christ.

CHAPTER 01

THE HUMAN CONDITION

"For all have sinned and fall short of the glory of God." - Romans 3:23

The Bible begins with a narrative of perfect harmony and fellowship between God and His creation. In the Garden of Eden, Adam and Eve lived in perfect communion with God, reflecting His glory and enjoying the fullness of life He intended for them. However, this idyllic state was shattered by an act of disobedience, introducing sin into the world and plunging humanity into darkness.

The concept of original sin is rooted in the story of Adam and Eve's fall. In Genesis 3, we read about the serpent's temptation and the subsequent disobedience of Adam and Eve. By eating the forbidden fruit, they chose to defy God's command, resulting in spiritual death and separation from God. This single act of rebellion had far-reaching consequences, affecting not only Adam and Eve but all their descendants.

Sin, in its essence, is a rebellion against God. It is the failure to live up to the standard of holiness and righteousness that God requires. Romans 3:23 succinctly captures this reality: "For all have sinned and fall short of the glory of God." This verse emphasizes the universality of sin; no one is exempt. Every human being, regardless of their background or circumstances, falls short of God's perfect standard.

The pervasive nature of sin is evident throughout the Bible. The prophet Isaiah declares, "All of us have become like one who is unclean, and all our righteous acts are like filthy rags" (Isaiah 64:6). This stark imagery highlights the futility of our efforts to attain righteousness on our own. Sin has tainted every aspect of our being, corrupting our thoughts, actions, and desires.

The consequences of sin are severe and far-reaching. Firstly, sin separates us from God. In Isaiah 59:2, we read, "But your iniquities have separated you from your God; your sins have hidden his face from you so that he will not hear." This separation is not merely a physical distance but a profound spiritual chasm that alienates us from the source of life and light.

Secondly, sin leads to spiritual death. The apostle Paul writes in Romans 6:23, "For the wages of sin is death." This death is not merely physical but encompasses spiritual death

— a state of being cut off from the life-giving presence of God. It is a condition of darkness, devoid of the light and hope that only God can provide.

Furthermore, sin affects our relationships with others. It breeds conflict, jealousy, and strife, leading to broken relationships and social discord. James 4:1-2 explains, "What causes fights and quarrels among you? Don't they come from your desires that battle within you? You desire but do not have, so you kill. You covet but you cannot get what you want, so you quarrel and fight." The selfish desires that stem from our sinful nature disrupt harmony and peace.

Given the pervasive nature of sin and its devastating consequences, humanity is in desperate need of redemption. Redemption, in a biblical sense, refers to the act of being saved or delivered from sin and its consequences. It is a divine intervention that restores us to a right relationship with God and brings us out of darkness into His marvelous light.

The universal need for redemption is highlighted throughout Scripture. In Romans 3:10-12, Paul writes, "As it is written: 'There is no one righteous, not even one; there is no one who understands; there is no one who seeks God. All have turned away, they have together become worthless; there is no one who does good, not even one.'" This passage underscores the total depravity of humanity and the inability to achieve righteousness apart from divine intervention.

Despite our sinful condition, God's love and grace shine brightly. From the moment of the fall, God set into motion His plan of redemption. In Genesis 3:15, we find the first hint of this plan: "And I will put enmity between you and the woman, and between your offspring and hers; he will crush your head, and you will strike his heel." This prophetic declaration points to the ultimate victory of Jesus Christ over sin and Satan.

The fulfillment of this promise is found in the person and work of Jesus Christ. John 1:29 records John the Baptist's proclamation upon seeing Jesus: "Look, the Lamb of God, who takes away the sin of the world!" Jesus, the sinless Son of God, came into the world to provide the redemption that humanity so desperately needs. His sacrificial death on the cross paid the penalty for our sins, and His resurrection conquered death, providing the way for us to be reconciled to God.

In Romans 5:18-19, Paul contrasts the disobedience of Adam with the obedience of Christ: "Consequently, just as one trespass resulted in condemnation for all people, so also one righteous act resulted in justification and life for all people. For just as through the disobedience of the one man the many were made sinners, so also through the obedience of the one man, the many will be made righteous." This passage highlights the profound impact of Christ's obedience and the gift of righteousness available to all who believe in Him.

Recognizing our need for redemption and understanding God's provision through Jesus Christ compels us to respond. The appropriate response is one of repentance and faith. Repentance involves acknowledging our sin, turning away from it, and seeking God's forgiveness. Acts 3:19 urges us, "Repent, then, and turn to God, so that your sins may be wiped out, that times of refreshing may come from the Lord."

Faith, on the other hand, involves trusting in Jesus Christ as our Savior and Lord. It is a wholehearted reliance on His finished work on the cross for our salvation. Ephesians 2:8-9 reminds us, "For it is by grace you have been saved, through faith – and this is not from yourselves, it is the gift of God – not by works so that no one can boast." Salvation is a gift that cannot be earned but must be received by faith.

As we embark on this theological journey from darkness to light, let us begin by acknowledging our brokenness and our need for redemption. Let us embrace the grace of God, who offers us forgiveness and new life through

Jesus Christ. And let us walk in the light of His truth, knowing that He has delivered us from the dominion of darkness and brought us into the kingdom of His beloved Son (Colossians 1:13).

May this chapter serve as a foundation for our exploration, setting the stage for the transformative truths that will guide us on our journey from darkness to light.

CHAPTER 02

THE PROMISE OF REDEMPTION

"For God so loved the world that he gave his one and only Son, that whoever believes in him shall not perish but have eternal life." - John 3:16

The promise of redemption is the central theme of the Christian faith. It is the beacon of hope that shines brightly in the midst of humanity's darkness. Redemption, in its simplest form, is the act of being saved from sin, error, or evil. This chapter delves into the heart of this promise, exploring the significance of God's love and grace in offering salvation through Jesus Christ. It is a journey from condemnation to liberation, from despair to eternal hope.

At the core of the promise of redemption is the profound love of God. John 3:16, perhaps the most well-known verse in the Bible, encapsulates this truth: "For God so loved the world that he gave his one and only Son, that whoever believes in him shall not perish but have eternal life."

The motivation for God's redemptive plan is His boundless love for humanity.

God's love is not contingent upon our worthiness or actions; it is an intrinsic part of His nature. The Apostle John emphasizes this in his first epistle, declaring, "God is love" (1 John 4:8). This love is sacrificial, self-giving, and unending. It reaches out to us even in our darkest moments, offering a way out of the mire of sin and into the light of His presence.

The Bible is replete with expressions of God's love. In Jeremiah 31:3, the Lord assures His people, "I have loved you with an everlasting love; I have drawn you with unfailing kindness." This everlasting love is not just an abstract concept but a tangible reality demonstrated through the person and work of Jesus Christ.

The promise of redemption is also rooted in the grace of God. Grace is the unmerited favor that God extends to humanity. It is a gift that we neither deserve nor can earn through our efforts. Ephesians 2:8-9 underscores this truth: "For it is by grace you have been saved, through faith – and this is not from yourselves, it is the gift of God – not by works so that no one can boast."

God's grace is vividly illustrated in the parable of the prodigal son (Luke 15:11-32). In this story, a wayward son squanders his inheritance and finds himself in desperate circumstances. When he decides to return home, expecting to be treated as a servant, his father runs to him, embraces him, and restores him as a son. This parable mirrors God's grace towards us. Despite our failures and sins, God welcomes us back with open arms, ready to forgive and restore us.

The Apostle Paul, in his letter to Titus, writes, "But when the kindness and love of God our Savior appeared, he saved us, not because of righteous things we had done, but because of his mercy. He saved us through the washing of rebirth and renewal by the Holy Spirit" (Titus 3:4-5). This passage highlights that our salvation is purely an act of God's mercy and grace.

The pinnacle of God's love and grace is found in the sacrificial death of Jesus Christ. Jesus, the Son of God, came into the world to fulfill the redemptive plan of the Father. His mission was to offer Himself as the perfect and final sacrifice for the sins of humanity.

The significance of Christ's sacrifice is profound. The writer of Hebrews explains, "For by one sacrifice he has made perfect forever those who are being made holy" (Hebrews 10:14). Jesus' death on the cross was not just a historical event; it was the culmination of God's redemptive plan, securing forgiveness and eternal life for all who believe in Him.

The concept of substitutionary atonement is central to understanding Christ's sacrifice. Isaiah 53:5-6 prophetically describes this: "But he was pierced for our transgressions, he was crushed for our iniquities; the punishment that brought us peace was on him, and by his wounds we are healed. We all, like sheep, have gone astray, each of us has turned to our own way; and the Lord has laid on him the iniquity of us all." Jesus took upon Himself the punishment that we deserved, offering us peace and healing in return.

The promise of redemption does not end with Christ's death; it is gloriously affirmed through His resurrection. The resurrection of Jesus is the cornerstone of the Christian faith, signifying victory over sin and death. Paul writes in 1 Corinthians 15:20-22, "But Christ has indeed been raised from the dead, the firstfruits of those who have fallen asleep. For since death came through a man, the resurrection of the dead comes also through a man. For as in Adam all die, so in Christ all will be made alive."

The resurrection assures us of eternal life. Jesus Himself declared, "I am the resurrection and the life. The one who believes in me will live, even though they die; and whoever lives by believing in me will never die" (John 11:25-26). This promise transforms our understanding of life and death, offering hope that extends beyond the grave.

The resurrection also empowers us to live victorious lives. Paul exclaims, "But thanks be to God! He gives us the victory through our Lord Jesus Christ" (1 Corinthians 15:57). This victory is not just future-oriented; it is a present reality. We are called to live in the power of the resurrected Christ, overcoming sin and walking in the newness of life.

The promise of redemption demands a response. It is an invitation to step out of darkness and into the light of God's love and grace. This response involves faith and repentance. To believe in Jesus Christ is to trust in His finished work on the cross and to acknowledge Him as Lord and Savior.

Faith is more than intellectual assent; it is a wholehearted commitment to follow Christ. Hebrews 11:1 defines faith as "confidence in what we hope for and assurance about what we do not see." This confidence is rooted in the reliability of God's promises and the transformative power of His grace.

Repentance, on the other hand, involves a turning away from sin and a turning towards God. It is a change of mind and heart that leads to a change in behavior. In Acts 3:19, Peter urges, "Repent, then, and turn to God, so that your sins may be wiped out, that times of refreshing may come from the Lord."

Accepting the promise of redemption is the beginning of a lifelong journey. It is a journey of growing in faith, experiencing God's grace, and becoming more like Christ. As we walk this path, we are continually transformed by the renewing of our minds and empowered by the Holy Spirit to live in the light.

The promise of redemption through Jesus Christ is the heart of the Gospel. It is the declaration that God's love and grace are greater than our sin and brokenness. Through the sacrificial death and triumphant resurrection of Jesus, we are offered forgiveness, restoration, and eternal life.

As we embrace this promise, let us respond with faith and repentance, stepping into the light of God's truth. Let us live as redeemed people, reflecting the love and grace we have received. And let us hold fast to the hope of eternal life, knowing that in Christ, we have been brought from darkness to light.

CHAPTER 03

THE JOURNEY OF FAITH

"Trust in the LORD with all your heart and lean not on your own understanding; in all your ways submit to him, and he will make your paths straight." - Proverbs 3:5-6

The journey of faith is a central theme in the Christian life. It is a path marked by trust, surrender, and the pursuit of God's will. Proverbs 3:5-6 serves as a guiding light for this journey, reminding us to trust in the Lord with all our heart, to refrain from leaning on our understanding, and to submit to Him in all our ways. This chapter delves into the essence of this journey, exploring its challenges and rewards as we strive toward the light.

Faith is the foundation of our relationship with God. Hebrews 11:1 defines faith as "confidence in what we hope for and assurance about what we do not see." This definition highlights two key aspects of faith: confidence and assurance. Faith is not merely wishful thinking; it is a deep-seated trust in the promises of God and a conviction of their reality, even when they are not visible to our natural eyes.

Faith is also relational. It involves placing our trust in the character and promises of God. The Bible is replete with examples of individuals who demonstrated remarkable faith. Abraham, known as the father of faith, believed in God's promise that he would become the father of many nations, even when it seemed impossible (Romans 4:18-21). His faith was counted by him as righteousness (Genesis 15:6).

Trust is a critical component of faith. Proverbs 3:5-6 exhorts us to "Trust in the LORD with all your heart." Trusting God involves relying on His wisdom, power, and goodness. It means believing that He is in control and that He has our best interests at heart. This trust is not partial or conditional; it is wholehearted and unwavering.

However, trusting God is not always easy. Life is filled with uncertainties, trials, and challenges that can shake our faith. In such times, we are tempted to rely on our own understanding and to seek solutions based on our limited perspective. Yet, the call to trust in the Lord is a call to surrender our need for control and to rest in the assurance that God is sovereign.

One of the greatest challenges to trusting God is the presence of suffering and evil in the world. When faced with pain and adversity, we may struggle to understand God's purposes. The story of Job is a poignant example of this struggle. Despite losing everything he held dear, Job ultimately declared, "Though he slay me, yet will I hope in him" (Job 13:15). His trust in God remained steadfast, even in the face of profound suffering.

Surrender is another essential aspect of the journey of faith. Proverbs 3:6 instructs us to "submit to him" in all our ways. Surrendering to God's will involves yielding our plans, desires, and ambitions to His purposes. It means allowing God to direct our paths and trusting that His ways are higher than our ways (Isaiah 55:8-9).

Jesus exemplified this surrender in the Garden of Gethsemane. As He faced the prospect of the cross, He prayed, "My Father, if it is possible, may this cup be taken from me. Yet not as I will, but as you will" (Matthew 26:39). Jesus' submission to the Father's will, even unto death, is the ultimate model of faith and surrender.

Surrendering to God's will often requires us to step out of our comfort zones and to take risks. Abraham's journey of faith began with a call to leave his homeland and to go to a land that God would show him (Genesis 12:1-4). This act of obedience required Abraham to trust in God's guidance, even when the destination was unknown.

Walking by faith is a dynamic and ongoing process. It involves daily decisions to trust and obey God. The Apostle Paul exhorts us to "walk by faith, not by sight" (2 Corinthians 5:7). This means living our lives based on the truth of God's Word and His promises, rather than on our circumstances or feelings.

Walking by faith also involves perseverance. The journey of faith is not always smooth; it is often marked by trials and testing. James 1:2-4 encourages us to "consider it pure joy… whenever you face trials of many kinds, because you know that the testing of your faith produces perseverance. Let perseverance finish its work so that you may be mature and complete, not lacking anything." Trials refine our faith, producing spiritual maturity and strengthening our reliance on God.

The story of the Israelites' journey from Egypt to the Promised Land illustrates the challenges of walking by faith. Despite witnessing God's miraculous deliverance and provision, the Israelites frequently faltered in their trust and obedience. Their journey was marked by moments of doubt, rebellion, and a longing to return to the familiar comforts of Egypt. Yet, through their wilderness wanderings, God remained faithful, guiding and sustaining them.

While the journey of faith can be challenging, it is also deeply rewarding. One of the primary rewards of faith is the deepening of our relationship with God. As we trust and surrender to Him, we experience His presence, guidance, and provision in our lives. Psalm 37:5-6 assures us, "Commit your way to the LORD; trust in him and he will do this: He will make your righteous reward shine like the dawn, your vindication like the noonday sun."

Faith also brings peace and joy. When we trust in God, we are freed from the anxieties and fears that come from relying on our own understanding. Philippians 4:6-7 encourages us, "Do not be anxious about anything, but in every situation, by prayer and petition, with thanksgiving, present your requests to God. And the peace of God, which transcends all understanding, will guard your hearts and your minds in Christ Jesus." This peace is a byproduct of a heart surrendered to God.

Moreover, faith leads to the fulfillment of God's promises. Throughout Scripture, we see that God rewards those who earnestly seek Him. Hebrews 11:6 states, "And without faith it is impossible to please God, because anyone who comes to him must believe that he exists and that he rewards those who earnestly seek him." The lives of the heroes of faith in Hebrews 11 testify to the reality that God honors and fulfills His promises to those who walk by faith.

The journey of faith is a profound and transformative path that requires trust, surrender, and perseverance. Proverbs 3:5-6 offers timeless wisdom for this journey, reminding us to trust in the Lord with all our heart, to lean not on our own understanding, and to submit to Him in all our ways. As we do so, we can be confident that God will make our paths straight, guiding us from darkness to light.

As we continue on this journey, let us embrace the challenges and rewards of walking by faith. Let us trust in God's character and promises, surrender our will to His purposes, and persevere through trials with the assurance that He is with us. May our journey of faith lead us ever closer to the light of God's presence, where we will find fullness of joy and eternal hope.

CHAPTER 04

THE POWER OF FORGIVENESS

"Bear with each other and forgive one another if any of you has a grievance against someone. Forgive as the Lord forgave you." - Colossians 3:13

Forgiveness is a central tenet of the Christian faith, embodying the grace and mercy that God extends to humanity. It holds transformative power, bringing healing and reconciliation to broken relationships and freeing us from the bondage of bitterness and resentment. In this chapter, we explore the profound impact of forgiveness, both in extending it to others and in receiving it from God. We will delve into the biblical basis for forgiveness and its role in our spiritual journey from darkness to light.

Colossians 3:13 exhorts us to "bear with each other and forgive one another if any of you has a grievance against someone. Forgive as the Lord forgave you." This command highlights the imperative nature of forgiveness in the life of a believer. Forgiveness is not optional; it is a reflection of the forgiveness we have received from God through Jesus Christ.

Jesus emphasized the importance of forgiveness in His teachings. In the Lord's Prayer, He instructed His disciples to pray, "Forgive us our debts, as we also have forgiven our debtors" (Matthew 6:12). This prayer underscores the reciprocal nature of forgiveness: we seek God's forgiveness while committing to forgive others. Jesus further reinforced this principle in Matthew 6:14-15, stating, "For if you forgive other people when they sin against you, your heavenly Father will also forgive you. But if you do not forgive others their sins, your Father will not forgive your sins."

The parable of the unforgiving servant (Matthew 18:21-35) powerfully illustrates the necessity of forgiveness. In the story, a servant who was forgiven a massive debt by his master refused to forgive a fellow servant a much smaller debt. When the master learned of this, he revoked his forgiveness and had the unforgiving servant punished. The parable teaches that those who have received forgiveness are expected to extend it to others.

Forgiveness has the power to transform individuals and relationships. It brings healing to wounds caused by betrayal, hurt, and offense. When we forgive, we release the hold that past grievances have on our lives, allowing us to move forward in freedom and peace.

One of the most profound examples of the transformative power of forgiveness is found in the story of Joseph. Sold into slavery by his brothers and later imprisoned under false accusations, Joseph had every reason to harbor bitterness and seek revenge. Yet, when he was reunited with his brothers, he chose to forgive them. He said, "You intended to harm me, but God intended it for good to accomplish what is now being done, the saving of many lives" (Genesis 50:20). Joseph's forgiveness not only restored his relationship with his brothers but also brought healing and reconciliation to his entire family.

Forgiveness also has the power to break the cycle of retaliation and violence. Jesus taught His followers to respond to offense with grace and forgiveness rather than seeking revenge. In Matthew 5:38-39, He said, "You have heard that it was said, 'Eye for eye, and tooth for tooth.' But I tell you, do not resist an evil person. If anyone slaps you on the right cheek, turn to them the other cheek also." By choosing forgiveness over retaliation, we interrupt the cycle of violence and create the possibility for reconciliation and peace.

Letting Go of Bitterness

Bitterness and unforgiveness are toxic to our souls. They consume our thoughts, damage our relationships, and hinder our spiritual growth. Ephesians 4:31-32 warns, "Get rid of all bitterness, rage and anger, brawling and slander, along with every form of malice. Be kind and compassionate to one another, forgiving each other, just as in Christ God forgave you." Letting go of bitterness is essential for our well-being and spiritual health.

The process of forgiveness often begins with a decision to release the offense and the offender. This decision is not based on feelings but on obedience to God's command. As we choose to forgive, we may still struggle with residual feelings of hurt and anger. It is important to bring these feelings to God in prayer, asking Him to heal our hearts and give us the grace to fully forgive.

Forgiveness does not mean condoning wrongdoing or forgetting the offense. It means releasing the desire for revenge and entrusting justice to God. Romans 12:19 reminds us, "Do not take revenge, my dear friends, but leave room for God's wrath, for it is written: 'It is mine to avenge; I will repay,' says the Lord." By releasing our grievances to God, we allow Him to be the righteous judge.

Just as we are called to forgive others, we must also embrace the forgiveness that God offers us. God's forgiveness is a gift of grace, made possible through the sacrifice of Jesus Christ. 1 John 1:9 assures us, "If we confess our sins, he is faithful and just and will forgive us our sins and purify us from all unrighteousness." When we repent and seek God's forgiveness, He removes our sins and restores us to a right relationship with Him.

The parable of the prodigal son (Luke 15:11-32) beautifully illustrates God's readiness to forgive. The younger son, having squandered his inheritance, returns home in repentance, expecting to be treated as a servant. Instead, his father runs to meet him, embraces him, and celebrates his return with a feast. This parable reveals the depth of God's love and His eagerness to forgive those who turn back to Him.

Embracing God's forgiveness also means accepting His grace for ourselves. Sometimes, we may find it difficult to forgive ourselves for past mistakes and failures. Yet, God's forgiveness is complete and unconditional. Psalm 103:12 declares, "As far as the east is from the west, so far has he removed our transgressions from us." When God forgives, He wipes the slate clean, offering us a fresh start.

Forgiveness opens the door to reconciliation. While forgiveness is a personal decision, reconciliation involves the restoration of relationships. It requires mutual willingness and effort from both parties. In some cases, reconciliation may not be possible or safe, particularly in situations of ongoing abuse or harm. However, whenever possible, forgiveness should lead to efforts towards healing and restoring broken relationships.

Matthew 18:15-17 provides a framework for seeking reconciliation. Jesus instructs us to address the offense privately with the person who has wronged us. If they do not listen, we are to involve one or two others as witnesses. If reconciliation still cannot be achieved, the matter may be brought before the church. This process underscores the importance of seeking peace and resolution within the Christian community.

Reconciliation also requires humility and a willingness to acknowledge our own faults. In Matthew 7:3-5, Jesus teaches, "Why do you look at the speck of sawdust in your brother's eye and pay no attention to the plank in your own eye? How can you say to your brother, 'Let me take the speck out of your eye,' when all the time there is a plank in your own eye? You hypocrite, first take the plank out of your own eye, and then you will see clearly to remove the speck from your brother's eye." True reconciliation involves self-examination and a readiness to seek and extend forgiveness.

Forgiveness brings freedom. It liberates us from the chains of anger, resentment, and bitterness. When we forgive, we experience a release of emotional and spiritual burdens. Jesus said, "Come to me, all you who are weary and burdened, and I will give you rest" (Matthew 11:28). Forgiveness is a means of entering into that rest, finding peace and healing in the presence of God.

The story of Corrie ten Boom offers a powerful testimony of the freedom found in forgiveness. After surviving a Nazi concentration camp, Corrie encountered one of her former guards who had since become a Christian. He asked for her forgiveness, and though she initially struggled, she chose to forgive him. In doing so, she experienced a profound sense of liberation and the transformative power of God's grace.

The power of forgiveness is a transformative force in our lives. It brings healing to our wounds, restores broken relationships, and frees us from the bondage of bitterness and resentment. As we extend forgiveness to others and embrace God's forgiveness for ourselves, we reflect the heart of the Gospel and move from darkness to light.

Let us heed the call of Colossians 3:13 to "bear with each other and forgive one another if any of you has a grievance against someone. Forgive as the Lord forgave you."

In doing so, we will experience the profound freedom and peace that come from living in the light of God's love and grace.

CHAPTER 05

WALKING IN THE LIGHT

"But if we walk in the light, as he is in the light, we have fellowship with one another, and the blood of Jesus, his Son, purifies us from all sin." - 1 John 1:7

Walking in the light of God's truth and righteousness is a profound and transformative journey. It involves aligning our lives with His Word, living in obedience to His commands, and reflecting His character in our daily actions. This chapter delves into the essence of walking in the light, examining the significance of living according to God's truth, the impact it has on our relationships, and the blessings that come from such a life.

To walk in the light means to live in a manner consistent with God's nature and truth. Light, in the Bible, is often associated with holiness, purity, and revelation. Jesus declared, "I am the light of the world. Whoever follows me will never walk in darkness, but will have the light of life"

(John 8:12). Walking in the light, therefore, is about following Jesus, the source of all truth and righteousness.

1 John 1:7 emphasizes that walking in the light brings fellowship with one another and purification from sin through the blood of Jesus. This verse highlights two key aspects of walking in the light: relational harmony and spiritual cleansing. As we live in the light, we experience deeper connections with fellow believers and ongoing sanctification through Christ's redemptive work.

Walking in the light requires a commitment to living according to God's Word. Psalm 119:105 declares, "Your word is a lamp for my feet, a light on my path." God's Word illuminates our way, providing guidance, wisdom, and direction for every aspect of our lives. By immersing ourselves in Scripture, we learn to discern God's will and to align our thoughts, attitudes, and actions with His truth.

Obedience to God's Word is a fundamental aspect of walking in the light. Jesus said, "If you love me, keep my commands" (John 14:15). Our love for God is demonstrated through our willingness to follow His instructions and to live by His standards. This obedience is not burdensome but a joyful response to His love and grace. As we obey God's Word, we grow in holiness and reflect His light to the world.

James 1:22-25 urges us to be "doers of the word, and not hearers only, deceiving yourselves." This passage underscores the importance of putting God's Word into practice. Hearing the Word without applying it leads to self-deception, but those who actively live out the Word are blessed in what they do. Walking in the light, therefore, involves both understanding and living out the truths of Scripture.

Walking in the light also means reflecting God's character in our daily lives. Ephesians 5:8-9 instructs, "For you were once darkness, but now you are light in the Lord. Live as children of light (for the fruit of the light consists in all goodness, righteousness and truth)." As children of light, we are called to exhibit the qualities of goodness, righteousness, and truth.

Goodness involves demonstrating kindness, compassion, and love towards others. Jesus taught that our love for one another is a testament to our discipleship: "By this everyone will know that you are my disciples, if you love one another" (John 13:35). As we walk in the light, our interactions with others should be marked by love and grace, reflecting the character of Christ.

Righteousness entails living with integrity and moral uprightness. It means making choices that honor God and uphold His standards. 1 Peter 1:15-16 calls us to holiness: "But just as he who called you is holy, so be holy in all you do; for it is written: 'Be holy, because I am holy.'" Walking in the light involves a commitment to righteousness in every area of our lives, seeking to please God in our thoughts, words, and actions.

Truth is foundational to walking in the light. Jesus declared, "I am the way and the truth and the life" (John 14:6). As followers of Christ, we are called to live in truth, rejecting falsehood and deception. This involves being honest in our dealings, speaking truthfully, and standing firm in the truth of God's Word. Ephesians 4:25 exhorts us, "Therefore each of you must put off falsehood and speak truthfully to your neighbor, for we are all members of one body."

Walking in the light profoundly impacts our relationships. 1 John 1:7 emphasizes that walking in the light leads to fellowship with one another. As we live in alignment with God's truth and reflect His character, we build authentic and healthy relationships within the body of Christ.

Walking in the light fosters unity and harmony among believers. Colossians 3:12-14 encourages us to "clothe yourselves with compassion, kindness, humility, gentleness and patience. Bear with each other and forgive one another if any of you has a grievance against someone. Forgive as the

Lord forgave you. And over all these virtues put on love, which binds them all together in perfect unity." These virtues are the fruit of walking in the light and contribute to strong, loving, and unified relationships.

Moreover, walking in the light enables us to be a witness to the world. Jesus taught, "You are the light of the world. A town built on a hill cannot be hidden. Neither do people light a lamp and put it under a bowl. Instead, they put it on its stand, and it gives light to everyone in the house. In the same way, let your light shine before others, that they may see your good deeds and glorify your Father in heaven" (Matthew 5:14-16). Our lives, when lived in the light, serve as a testimony to God's transforming power, drawing others to Him.

Walking in the light brings manifold blessings. One of the foremost blessings is purification from sin. 1 John 1:7 assures us that "the blood of Jesus, his Son, purifies us from all sin." As we walk in the light, we experience ongoing cleansing and sanctification through the sacrificial blood of Christ. This purification is not a one-time event but a continuous process of being made holy.

Another blessing of walking in the light is the deep sense of peace and security that comes from living in alignment with God's will. Psalm 119:165 declares, "Great peace have those who love your law, and nothing can make them stumble." Obedience to God's Word brings peace to our hearts, guarding us from the turmoil and confusion that result from living in darkness.

Walking in the light also brings clarity and purpose to our lives. Proverbs 4:18 promises, "The path of the righteous is like the morning sun, shining ever brighter till the full light of day." As we walk in the light, our path becomes clearer, and our understanding of God's purpose for our lives grows. We are able to navigate life's challenges with confidence, knowing that God is directing our steps.

Finally, walking in the light leads to an intimate fellowship with God. John 14:23 records Jesus' promise: "Anyone who loves me will obey my teaching. My Father will love them, and we will come to them and make our home with them." Obedience to God's Word invites His presence into our lives, deepening our relationship with Him and allowing us to experience His love and guidance more fully.

Walking in the light is a journey of living in alignment with God's truth, reflecting His character, and experiencing the blessings of obedience. As we commit to walking in the light, we build authentic relationships, witness to the world, and enjoy the peace, clarity, and fellowship that come from living according to God's Word.

1 John 1:7 reminds us of the profound impact of walking in the light: "But if we walk in the light, as he is in the light, we have fellowship with one another, and the blood of Jesus, his Son, purifies us from all sin." Let us strive to walk in the light, embracing the transformative power of God's truth and allowing His light to shine through us. In doing so, we move ever closer to the fullness of life that God desires for us, stepping out of darkness and into the glorious light of His presence.

CHAPTER 06

OVERCOMING TRIALS

"I have told you these things, so that in me you may have peace. In this world, you will have trouble. But take heart! I have overcome the world." - John 16:33

Trials and suffering are inevitable parts of the human experience. Jesus Himself acknowledged this reality, but He also offered a profound assurance: in Him, we find peace and victory. This chapter explores the nature of trials, the role they play in our spiritual growth, and the assurance of God's presence and triumph in the midst of adversity.

Jesus' words in John 16:33 make it clear that we will face trouble in this world. The Greek word for "trouble" here is thlipsis, which denotes pressure, distress, and affliction. Trials can take many forms—illness, loss, financial difficulties, relational conflicts, and more. They are part and parcel of life in a fallen world.

James 1:2-4 further emphasizes this reality: "Consider it pure joy, my brothers and sisters, whenever you face trials of many kinds, because you know that the testing of your faith produces perseverance. Let perseverance finish its work so that you may be mature and complete, not lacking anything." The apostle James encourages believers to view trials not as random misfortunes but as opportunities for growth and maturity.

The apostle Peter also addresses the certainty of suffering: "Dear friends, do not be surprised at the fiery ordeal that has come on you to test you, as though something strange was happening to you" (1 Peter 4:12). Rather than being taken aback by trials, we are called to recognize them as part of the Christian journey.

One of the most comforting truths in the face of trials is the assurance of God's presence. Psalm 23:4 declares, "Even though I walk through the darkest valley, I will fear no evil, for you are with me; your rod and your staff, they comfort me." God's presence brings comfort, guidance, and protection, even in the darkest times.

In Isaiah 43:2, God promises, "When you pass through the waters, I will be with you; and when you pass through the rivers, they will not sweep over you. When you walk through the fire, you will not be burned; the flames will not set you ablaze." This verse reassures us that God does not abandon us in our trials. Instead, He walks with us, ensuring that we are not overwhelmed or destroyed by the hardships we face.

Jesus' promise in Matthew 28:20 is particularly powerful: "And surely I am with you always, to the very end of the age." This enduring presence of Christ provides a source of unwavering hope and strength, enabling us to face trials with confidence and courage.

Trials serve a refining purpose in our lives. They are not merely obstacles to be endured but are instrumental in shaping our character and faith. 1 Peter 1:6-7 explains, "In all this you greatly rejoice, though now for a little while you may have had to suffer grief in all kinds of trials. These have come so that the proven genuineness of your faith—of greater worth than gold, which perishes even though refined by fire—may result in praise, glory and honor when Jesus Christ is revealed."

Just as gold is refined by fire to remove impurities, our faith is refined through trials. This refining process strengthens our trust in God, deepens our dependence on Him, and produces perseverance. Romans 5:3-5 echoes this truth: "Not only so, but we also glory in our sufferings, because we know that suffering produces perseverance;

perseverance, character; and character, hope. And hope does not put us to shame, because God's love has been poured out into our hearts through the Holy Spirit, who has been given to us."

Job's story is a profound example of this refining process. Despite immense suffering, Job remained steadfast in his faith. In Job 23:10, he declares, "But he knows the way that I take; when he has tested me, I will come forth as gold." Job's perseverance through trials led to a deeper revelation of God and a renewed faith.

Trials often expose our weaknesses and limitations, but they also provide an opportunity for God's strength to be displayed in our lives. The apostle Paul experienced this firsthand. In 2 Corinthians 12:9-10, he writes, "But he said to me, 'My grace is sufficient for you, for my power is made perfect in weakness.' Therefore I will boast all the more gladly about my weaknesses, so that Christ's power may rest on me. That is why, for Christ's sake, I delight in weaknesses, in insults, in hardships, in persecutions, in difficulties. For when I am weak, then I am strong."

Paul's thorn in the flesh, a persistent trial, revealed his dependence on God's grace. Rather than removing the trial, God provided Paul with the strength to endure it, demonstrating that divine power is perfected in human weakness. This principle applies to all believers: our trials highlight our need for God and provide a platform for His strength to be manifested in our lives.

Isaiah 40:29-31 beautifully captures this truth: "He gives strength to the weary and increases the power of the weak. Even youths grow tired and weary, and young men stumble and fall, but those who hope in the Lord will renew their strength. They will soar on wings like eagles; they will run and not grow weary, they will walk and not be faint." God's strength is available to us in our trials, enabling us to rise above our circumstances and continue moving forward.

Ultimately, the greatest assurance we have in the face of trials is the victory that has been secured through Jesus Christ. In John 16:33, Jesus offers these comforting words: "I have told you these things, so that in me you may have peace. In this world, you will have trouble. But take heart! I have overcome the world." Jesus' victory over sin, death, and the powers of darkness guarantees our triumph.

Romans 8:35-37 further reinforces this assurance: "Who shall separate us from the love of Christ? Shall trouble or hardship or persecution or famine or nakedness or danger or sword? As it is written: 'For your sake we face death all day long; we are considered as sheep to be slaughtered.' No, in all these things we are more than conquerors through him who loved us." Through Christ, we are more than conquerors, able to face any trial with confidence in His ultimate victory.

The book of Revelation offers a glorious vision of this victory. Revelation 21:4 proclaims, "'He will wipe every tear from their eyes. There will be no more death' or mourning or crying or pain, for the old order of things has passed away." This promise of a future free from suffering and filled with eternal joy sustains us through our present trials.

Trials and suffering are inevitable in this world, but we are not without hope. God's presence with us in the midst of trials, the refining purpose they serve, the display of His strength in our weakness, and the assurance of victory through Christ all provide a solid foundation for overcoming adversity.

Jesus' words in John 16:33 remind us to take heart and find peace in Him, for He has overcome the world. As we navigate the trials of life, let us hold fast to this assurance, trusting in God's faithfulness and allowing Him to lead us from darkness to light. In doing so, we experience the transformative power of His presence and emerge stronger, more resilient, and more deeply rooted in our faith.

CHAPTER 07

THE HOPE OF RESURRECTION

"Jesus said to her, 'I am the resurrection and the life. The one who believes in me will live, even though they die; and whoever lives by believing in me will never die. Do you believe this?'" - John 11:25-26

The hope of resurrection and eternal life is one of the most profound and comforting promises in the Christian faith. In this chapter, we will delve into the significance of Christ's victory over death, the assurance it brings to believers, and the transformative power of living in the light of resurrection hope.

The resurrection of Jesus Christ stands as the cornerstone of the Christian faith. His victory over death is not just an event in history but the foundation of our hope and assurance. In 1 Corinthians 15:20-22, the apostle Paul declares, "But Christ has indeed been raised from the dead, the firstfruits of those who have fallen asleep. For since death came through a man, the resurrection of the dead comes also through a man. For as in Adam all die, so in Christ all will be made alive."

Through His resurrection, Jesus conquered death, breaking its power and providing a pathway to eternal life. This victory is not just for Him alone but extends to all who believe in Him. By calling Himself "the resurrection and the life," Jesus assures us that through faith in Him, we too will experience resurrection and eternal life.

Jesus' conversation with Martha in John 11:25-26 offers profound reassurance. When Jesus declares, "I am the resurrection and the life," He is not only asserting His power over death but also inviting us to place our trust in Him. This invitation comes with a promise: "The one who believes in me will live, even though they die; and whoever lives by believing in me will never die."

This assurance of eternal life transforms our understanding of death. For believers, death is not the end but a transition into a new and eternal life with God. The fear and finality of death are replaced with hope and anticipation. As Paul writes in Philippians 1:21, "For to me, to live is Christ and to die is gain." This perspective allows believers to face death with confidence, knowing that it leads to eternal life in the presence of God.

In 1 Thessalonians 4:13-14, Paul provides further encouragement: "Brothers and sisters, we do not want you to be uninformed about those who sleep in death, so that you do not grieve like the rest of mankind, who have no hope. For we believe that Jesus died and rose again, and so we believe that God will bring with Jesus those who have fallen asleep in him." This passage highlights the hope we have in the resurrection, assuring us that we will be reunited with our loved ones who have died in Christ.

Living in the light of resurrection hope profoundly impacts our lives. It shifts our focus from the temporal to the eternal and from earthly struggles to heavenly promises. Colossians 3:1-2 exhorts us, "Since, then, you have been raised with Christ, set your hearts on things above, where Christ is, seated at the right hand of God. Set your minds on things above, not on earthly things." This eternal perspective transforms our values, priorities, and behaviors.

The hope of resurrection empowers us to live boldly and sacrificially for Christ. In 1 Corinthians 15:58, Paul encourages believers, "Therefore, my dear brothers and sisters, stand firm. Let nothing move you. Always give yourselves fully to the work of the Lord, because you know that your labor in the Lord is not in vain." Knowing that our future is secure in Christ gives us the courage to persevere in faith and service, even in the face of difficulties and opposition.

Resurrection hope also brings comfort in times of suffering and loss. In Romans 8:18, Paul writes, "I consider that our present sufferings are not worth comparing with the glory that will be revealed in us." The promise of future glory outweighs our present hardships, providing a source of strength and endurance. This hope allows us to endure trials with the assurance that a greater and eternal joy awaits us.

The resurrection of Jesus is not only a past event but also a foretaste of the future glory that awaits all believers. In 1 Corinthians 15:42-44, Paul describes the resurrection body: "So will it be with the resurrection of the dead. The body that is sown is perishable, it is raised imperishable; it is sown in dishonor, it is raised in glory; it is sown in weakness, it is raised in power; it is sown a natural body, it is raised a spiritual body."

Our resurrection bodies will be imperishable, glorious, powerful, and spiritual—far surpassing our current physical limitations. This transformation is part of the new creation that God is bringing about, where sin, death, and suffering will be no more. Revelation 21:4 gives us a glimpse of this future: "He will wipe every tear from their eyes. There will be no more death or mourning or crying or pain, for the old order of things has passed away."

The hope of resurrection also compels us to live in anticipation of Christ's return. In Titus 2:13, Paul speaks of "the blessed hope—the appearing of the glory of our great God and Savior, Jesus Christ." This blessed hope fuels our perseverance, holiness, and mission, as we eagerly await the fulfillment of God's redemptive plan.

Jesus' question to Martha, "Do you believe this?" is a question that each of us must answer. Belief in the resurrection and eternal life is not just an intellectual assent but a transformative faith that shapes our lives and destinies. John 5:24 records Jesus' words: "Very truly I tell you, whoever hears my word and believes him who sent me has eternal life and will not be judged but has crossed over from death to life."

This invitation to believe and receive eternal life is extended to all. In Romans 10:9, Paul outlines the simple yet profound step of faith: "If you declare with your mouth, 'Jesus is Lord,' and believe in your heart that God raised him from the dead, you will be saved." This belief ushers us into a new life in Christ, marked by the hope of resurrection and the promise of eternal fellowship with God.

The hope of resurrection and eternal life in Jesus Christ is a cornerstone of the Christian faith. It assures us of victory over death, transforms our perspective on life and suffering, and compels us to live in anticipation of future glory. Jesus' victory over death is not just a historical event but a present reality that infuses our lives with hope, purpose, and eternal significance.

As we reflect on Jesus' words in John 11:25-26, let us embrace the hope of resurrection with unwavering faith. This hope anchors our souls, sustains us through trials, and guides us from darkness to light. With the assurance of eternal life, we can face the future with confidence, knowing that in Christ, death has been defeated, and life everlasting awaits us.

CHAPTER 08

EMBRACING GRACE

"But he said to me, 'My grace is sufficient for you, for my power is made perfect in weakness.' Therefore, I will boast all the more gladly about my weaknesses, so that Christ's power may rest on me." - 2 Corinthians 12:9

The concept of grace is at the heart of the Christian faith. It is through grace that we are saved, sustained, and empowered to live victoriously. This chapter examines the boundless grace of God, how it covers our shortcomings, and its transformative impact on our lives. We will explore the beauty of God's unmerited favor and how embracing this grace leads us from darkness to light.

Grace, at its core, is the unmerited favor of God. It is a gift that we neither earn nor deserve. Ephesians 2:8-9 states, "For it is by grace you have been saved, through faith—and this is not from yourselves, it is the gift of God—not by works, so that no one can boast." This passage underscores that grace is a divine gift, freely given by God out of His love and mercy.

The Greek word for grace, charis, conveys the idea of kindness and favor bestowed without expectation of return. This grace is evident throughout Scripture, from God's patience with Israel despite their rebellion to Jesus' sacrificial death on the cross. Romans 5:8 encapsulates this truth: "But God demonstrates his own love for us in this: While we were still sinners, Christ died for us." Grace is God's proactive love reaching out to us, even when we are undeserving.

One of the most comforting aspects of grace is its ability to cover our shortcomings. In Romans 3:23-24, Paul writes, "For all have sinned and fall short of the glory of God, and all are justified freely by his grace through the redemption that came by Christ Jesus." Our sins and failures are not the final word; grace is. Through the redemption provided by Jesus, we are justified and made right with God.

This covering of grace is vividly illustrated in the parable of the prodigal son (Luke 15:11-32). Despite his rebellion and waywardness, the prodigal son is welcomed back by his father with open arms and a celebratory feast. This parable demonstrates the depth of God's grace—His willingness to forgive and restore us, no matter how far we have strayed.

Psalm 103:12 beautifully describes this covering: "As far as the east is from the west, so far has he removed our transgressions from us." When we embrace God's grace, our sins are removed and we are clothed in His righteousness, allowing us to stand before Him blameless and pure.

Grace is not just about covering our sins; it also empowers us to live victoriously. In 2 Corinthians 12:9, Paul shares a profound revelation: "But he said to me, 'My grace is sufficient for you, for my power is made perfect in weakness.' Therefore, I will boast all the more gladly about my weaknesses, so that Christ's power may rest on me." Paul's experience of grace teaches us that it is in our weaknesses that God's power is most evident.

This empowerment through grace is a recurring theme in Paul's writings. In Philippians 4:13, he declares, "I can do all this through him who gives me strength." The strength to overcome obstacles, endure hardships, and fulfill God's purposes in our lives comes from His grace. It is a source of divine power that enables us to rise above our limitations and live in victory.

Titus 2:11-12 further illustrates this empowering grace: "For the grace of God has appeared that offers salvation to all people. It teaches us to say 'No' to ungodliness and worldly passions, and to live self-controlled, upright and godly lives in this present age." Grace not only saves us but also instructs and enables us to live in a manner that honors God. It is a transformative force that shapes our character and behavior.

The beauty of grace lies in its unmerited nature. It is a reflection of God's character—His love, mercy, and compassion. Grace is beautifully depicted in the story of the woman caught in adultery (John 8:1-11). The religious leaders were ready to stone her, but Jesus responded with grace. He challenged the accusers, saying, "Let any one of you who is without sin be the first to throw a stone at her." When they all left, Jesus told the woman, "Neither do I condemn you. Go now and leave your life of sin." This act of grace not only spared her life but also offered her a new beginning.

Grace is also evident in the calling of the apostle Paul. Formerly Saul, a persecutor of Christians, Paul experienced God's grace on the road to Damascus (Acts 9:1-19). Despite his past, God chose him to be an apostle and a key figure in the early church. Paul's life and ministry are testaments to the transformative power of grace, turning a persecutor into a proclaimer of the gospel.

Embracing grace has a profound and transformative impact on our lives. It changes how we view ourselves, others, and our relationship with God. Grace fosters humility, gratitude, and a deep sense of dependence on God. It also compels us to extend grace to others, as we have freely received it.

In Colossians 3:12-13, Paul instructs, "Therefore, as God's chosen people, holy and dearly loved, clothe yourselves with compassion, kindness, humility, gentleness and patience. Bear with each other and forgive one another if any of you has a grievance against someone. Forgive as the Lord forgave you." Grace begets grace. As recipients of God's unmerited favor, we are called to show the same grace to those around us, fostering a community marked by love and forgiveness.

Grace also transforms our understanding of service. In 1 Peter 4:10, Peter writes, "Each of you should use whatever gift you have received to serve others, as faithful stewards of God's grace in its various forms." Our talents and abilities are gifts of grace, entrusted to us for the purpose of serving others and glorifying God. Embracing grace leads us to steward these gifts faithfully, recognizing that they are given by God and should be used for His purposes.

Living in the light of grace means embracing our identity as beloved children of God, redeemed and empowered by His grace. It means walking in humility, recognizing our need for God's grace daily. It means extending grace to others, reflecting God's love and mercy in our interactions.

Hebrews 4:16 encourages us to approach God with confidence because of His grace: "Let us then approach God's throne of grace with confidence, so that we may receive mercy and find grace to help us in our time of need." This invitation to draw near to God with boldness is a powerful reminder of the accessibility and sufficiency of His grace. No matter our struggles or failures, we can always come to God and find grace to sustain and strengthen us.

The boundless grace of God is a central theme of the Christian faith. It covers our shortcomings, empowers us to live victoriously, and transforms our lives. Embracing grace means accepting God's unmerited favor and allowing it to shape our identity, actions, and relationships.

As we reflect on 2 Corinthians 12:9, let us remember that God's grace is sufficient for us. In our weaknesses, His power is made perfect. By embracing this grace, we move from darkness to light, experiencing the transformative impact of God's unending love and favor. With hearts full of gratitude and humility, let us live in the light of grace, extending it to others and glorifying God in all that we do.

CHAPTER 09

THE CALL TO HOLINESS

"But just as he who called you is holy, so be holy in all you do; for it is written: 'Be holy because I am holy.'" - 1 Peter 1:15-16

The call to holiness is a profound and essential aspect of the Christian journey. It is an invitation to reflect God's character and glory through our lives. This chapter explores the biblical call to holiness, the process of sanctification, and the practical implications of living a life set apart for God's purposes.

Holiness is a central theme throughout the Bible, beginning with God's revelation of Himself as holy. In Isaiah 6:3, the seraphim declares, "Holy, holy, holy is the LORD Almighty; the whole earth is full of his glory." God's holiness signifies His absolute purity, moral perfection, and separation from sin.

In the Old Testament, God called Israel to be a holy nation, set apart for His purposes. Leviticus 19:2 commands, "Speak to the entire assembly of Israel and say to them: 'Be holy because I, the LORD your God, am holy.'" This call was not just about ritual purity but about living in a manner that reflected God's character.

The New Testament continues this theme, emphasizing that believers are called to holiness. In 1 Peter 1:15-16, the apostle Peter urges Christians to be holy in all they do, echoing the command from Leviticus. This call to holiness is rooted in our relationship with God and our identity as His children.

Sanctification is the process of being made holy, set apart for God's purposes. It is both an instantaneous and ongoing work in the life of a believer. At the moment of salvation, we are positionally sanctified, declared holy and righteous before God through the sacrifice of Jesus Christ. Hebrews 10:10 states, "And by that will, we have been made holy through the sacrifice of the body of Jesus Christ once and for all."

However, sanctification is also a progressive process, where we grow in holiness and Christlikeness over time. Philippians 1:6 assures us, "being confident of this, that he who began a good work in you will carry it on to completion until the day of Christ Jesus." The Holy Spirit plays a crucial role in this process, transforming us from within and enabling us to live in accordance with God's will.

Living a life of holiness involves intentional choices and actions that align with God's character and purposes. It requires us to turn away from sin and pursue righteousness. Romans 12:1-2 provides a practical framework for this pursuit: "Therefore, I urge you, brothers and sisters, in view of God's mercy, to offer your bodies as a living sacrifice, holy and pleasing to God—this is your true and proper worship. Do not conform to the pattern of this world, but be transformed by the renewing of your mind."

Offering our bodies as living sacrifices means dedicating every aspect of our lives to God. It involves our thoughts, words, actions, and relationships. This holistic approach to holiness requires a daily commitment to seek God's will and to allow His Word to shape our lives.

Holiness is ultimately about reflecting God's character in our lives. As we grow in holiness, we exhibit attributes such as love, kindness, patience, humility, and integrity. Colossians 3:12-14 exhorts us, "Therefore, as God's chosen people, holy and dearly loved, clothe yourselves with compassion, kindness, humility, gentleness and patience. Bear with each other and forgive one another if any of you has a grievance against someone. Forgive as the Lord forgave you. And over all these virtues put on love, which binds them all together in perfect unity."

These virtues are not just moral duties but expressions of God's character. By embodying these qualities, we bear witness to God's holiness and draw others to Him.

The Holy Spirit is essential in our journey towards holiness. He convicts us of sin, empowers us to overcome it, and guides us in truth. Galatians 5:16-17 encourages us, "So I say, walk by the Spirit, and you will not gratify the desires of the flesh. For the flesh desires what is contrary to the Spirit, and the Spirit what is contrary to the flesh. They are in conflict with each other, so that you are not to do whatever you want."

Walking by the Spirit means yielding to His influence and allowing Him to lead our lives. It involves daily surrender and reliance on His power to live in a manner that pleases God.

Holiness is not confined to religious activities but permeates every aspect of our lives. It affects our work, relationships, leisure, and even our thoughts. Colossians 3:17 instructs, "And whatever you do, whether in word or deed, do it all in the name of the Lord Jesus, giving thanks to God the Father through him."

In the workplace, holiness means integrity, diligence, and treating others with respect. In our relationships, it means love, forgiveness, and selflessness. In our leisure, it means choosing activities that honor God and align with His values.

Living a life of holiness brings profound rewards. Firstly, it deepens our relationship with God. Matthew 5:8 promises, "Blessed are the pure in heart, for they will see God." As we pursue holiness, we experience greater intimacy with God and a clearer understanding of His will.

Secondly, holiness brings peace and joy. Psalm 1:1-2 describes the blessedness of those who delight in God's law: "Blessed is the one who does not walk in step with the wicked or stand in the way that sinners take or sit in the company of mockers, but whose delight is in the law of the LORD, and who meditates on his law day and night." A life aligned with God's will leads to inner peace and fulfillment.

Our holiness also impacts the world around us. As we reflect God's character, we become a light in the darkness, drawing others to Him. Jesus emphasized this in Matthew 5:14-16: "You are the light of the world. A town built on a hill cannot be hidden. Neither do people light a lamp and put it under a bowl. Instead, they put it on its stand, and it gives light to everyone in the house. In the same way, let your light shine before others, that they may see your good deeds and glorify your Father in heaven."

Our holiness serves as a testimony to God's transforming power and invites others to experience His grace and love.

The call to holiness is a vital and beautiful aspect of our Christian journey. It is an invitation to reflect God's character, live in a manner that honors Him, and impact the world for His glory. As we embrace this call, we grow in our relationship with God, experience the blessings of a holy life, and become a beacon of light in a dark world.

Let us heed the call of 1 Peter 1:15-16, striving to be holy in all we do, just as our Heavenly Father is holy. By His grace and the power of the Holy Spirit, we can live lives that reflect His glory and draw others to the light of His love.

CHAPTER 10

THE ETERNAL LIGHT

"The city does not need the sun or the moon to shine on it, for the glory of God gives it light, and the Lamb is its lamp." - Revelation 21:23

The journey from darkness to light finds its ultimate fulfillment in the eternal presence of God. The promise of eternal light, described in the book of Revelation, provides a vision of the future that transcends the trials and tribulations of this life. This final chapter explores the beauty and majesty of dwelling in God's presence for eternity, where there is no more darkness, pain, or sorrow.

In the book of Revelation, the apostle John is given a vision of the New Jerusalem, a city where God's glory illuminates everything. Revelation 21:2-4 paints a picture of this glorious future: "I saw the Holy City, the new Jerusalem, coming down out of heaven from God, prepared as a bride beautifully dressed for her husband. And I heard a loud voice from the throne saying, 'Look! God's dwelling place is now among the people, and he will dwell with them. They will be his people, and God himself will be with them and be their God. He will wipe every tear from their eyes. There will be no more death or mourning or crying or pain, for the old order of things has passed away.'"

This vision encapsulates the hope and promise of eternity with God. The New Jerusalem represents a restored creation where the brokenness of this world is replaced by the perfection of God's kingdom.

One of the most striking images in this vision is that of God's glory providing light. Revelation 21:23 declares, "The city does not need the sun or the moon to shine on it, for the glory of God gives it light, and the Lamb is its lamp." This signifies the complete and utter presence of God, rendering all other sources of light unnecessary. The Lamb, Jesus Christ, is the lamp, signifying His central role in our redemption and eternal life.

In this eternal city, there is no more darkness—literal or metaphorical. The absence of night symbolizes the end of sin, evil, and suffering. Revelation 22:5 reiterates, "There will be no more night. They will not need the light of a lamp or the light of the sun, for the Lord God will give them light. And they will reign forever and ever."

The eternal light of God's presence also signifies the end of all suffering and sorrow. Revelation 21:4 reassures us that "He will wipe every tear from their eyes. There will be no more death or mourning or crying or pain, for the old order of things has passed away." The promise of no more pain, sorrow, or death is a profound comfort to believers who endure trials and tribulations in this life.

This promise is grounded in the victory of Jesus Christ over sin and death. His resurrection is the guarantee of our future resurrection and the transformation of all creation. 1 Corinthians 15:54-55 proclaims, "When the perishable has been clothed with the imperishable, and the mortal with immortality, then the saying that is written will come true: 'Death has been swallowed up in victory.' 'Where, O death, is your victory? Where, O death, is your sting?'"

Dwelling in the eternal light means living in the unmediated presence of God. Revelation 22:3-4 describes this intimate relationship: "No longer will there be any curse. The throne of God and of the Lamb will be in the city, and his servants will serve him. They will see his face, and his name will be on their foreheads." Seeing God's face signifies a direct and personal relationship with Him, unencumbered by the barriers of sin and mortality.

This eternal presence fulfills the deepest longings of the human heart. Psalm 16:11 declares, "You make known to me the path of life; you will fill me with joy in your presence, with eternal pleasures at your right hand." The joy and satisfaction found in God's presence surpass all earthly experiences.

The eternal light of God's presence also encompasses eternal worship and reign. Revelation 22:3 indicates that "his servants will serve him," suggesting a life of joyful service and worship. This service is not burdensome but a fulfillment of our true purpose, as Revelation 22:5 notes, "And they will reign forever and ever."

Worship in eternity is described in Revelation 5:13-14, where every creature in heaven and on earth joins in a chorus of praise: "Then I heard every creature in heaven and on earth and under the earth and on the sea, and all that is in them, saying: 'To him who sits on the throne and to the Lamb be praise and honor and glory and power, forever and ever!' The four living creatures said, 'Amen,' and the elders fell down and worshiped."

The vision of the eternal light is not just a distant future but an invitation to live in the light of God's presence now. Jesus, the Light of the World, calls us to follow Him and walk in His light. John 8:12 records Jesus' words: "I am the light of the world. Whoever follows me will never walk in darkness, but will have the light of life."

Living in the light involves daily surrender to Christ, allowing His Word to guide our steps and His Spirit to transform our hearts. Ephesians 5:8-10 exhorts, "For you were once darkness, but now you are light in the Lord. Live as children of light (for the fruit of the light consists in all goodness, righteousness, and truth) and find out what pleases the Lord."

The journey from darkness to light culminates in the eternal presence of God, where His glory illuminates everything and His love eradicates all pain and sorrow. This vision of the New Jerusalem fills us with hope and anticipation, encouraging us to persevere in faith and holiness.

As we live in the light of Christ today, we are reminded that our ultimate destination is a place where darkness is no more, where we will dwell with God forever, basking in His eternal light and love. Revelation 22:20-21 concludes with a fitting prayer, "He who testifies to these things says, 'Yes, I am coming soon.' Amen. Come, Lord Jesus. The grace of the Lord Jesus is with God's people. Amen."

Let us embrace this promise and live each day in the light of God's presence, anticipating the glorious day when we will see Him face to face and dwell with Him for eternity.

CHAPTER 11

LIVING IN THE LIGHT

"For you were once darkness, but now you are light in the Lord. Live as children of light." - Ephesians 5:8

The journey from darkness to light is not merely a destination but a way of life. As believers, we are called to live as children of light, embodying the transformative power of the gospel in our daily lives. This chapter explores what it means to live in the light, the practical implications of walking in God's truth, and the impact it has on our relationships and the world around us.

In his letter to the Ephesians, the Apostle Paul reminds believers of their new identity in Christ: "For you were once darkness, but now you are light in the Lord. Live as children of light" (Ephesians 5:8). This call to be light is both a privilege and a responsibility. As recipients of God's grace, we are transformed from darkness to light, and we are to reflect that light in every aspect of our lives.

Living in the light involves a conscious and continuous effort to align our thoughts, actions, and attitudes with God's will. It means rejecting the deeds of darkness and embracing the virtues of goodness, righteousness, and truth. Ephesians 5:9-10 further instructs us, "For the fruit of the light consists in all goodness, righteousness, and truth and find out what pleases the Lord."

Integrity is a cornerstone of living in the light. It involves being honest, trustworthy, and consistent in our actions, whether in public or private. Proverbs 10:9 states, "Whoever walks in integrity walks securely, but whoever takes crooked paths will be found out." Integrity builds a solid foundation for our relationships and enables us to be credible witnesses of Christ's transformative power.

Living in the light also means being transparent and accountable. James 5:16 encourages believers to "confess your sins to each other and pray for each other so that you may be healed. The prayer of a righteous person is powerful and effective." By being open about our struggles and seeking support from our faith community, we foster an environment of mutual growth and healing.

One of the most profound ways to live in the light is by reflecting Christ's love to others. Jesus taught that the greatest commandments are to love God with all our heart, soul, mind, and strength and to love our neighbors as ourselves (Mark 12:30-31). This love is not merely an emotion but a deliberate choice to act with compassion, kindness, and selflessness.

1 John 4:7-8 emphasizes the importance of love: "Dear friends, let us love one another, for love comes from God. Everyone who loves has been born of God and knows God. Whoever does not love does not know God, because God is love." By loving others as Christ loves us, we become beacons of His light, drawing people to Him.

Good works are a natural outflow of living in the light. Ephesians 2:10 reminds us, "For we are God's handiwork, created in Christ Jesus to do good works, which God prepared in advance for us to do." These good works are not a means to earn salvation but a response to the grace we have received.

Engaging in good works involves serving others, advocating for justice, and meeting the needs of those around us. Matthew 5:16 encourages us, "In the same way, let your light shine before others, that they may see your good deeds and glorify your Father in heaven." Our actions can inspire others to seek the light and glorify God.

Living in the light also means actively opposing the forces of darkness. Romans 12:21 exhorts us, "Do not be overcome by evil, but overcome evil with good." As children of light, we are called to stand against injustice, corruption, and sin, using the power of truth and righteousness.

This can be challenging, as the world is often hostile to the light. John 3:19-21 explains, "This is the verdict: Light has come into the world, but people loved darkness instead of light because their deeds were evil. Everyone who does evil hates the light and will not come into the light for fear that their deeds will be exposed. But whoever lives by the truth comes into the light, so that it may be seen plainly that what they have done has been done in the sight of God."

Despite opposition, we must remain steadfast, relying on God's strength and guidance. Philippians 2:15 encourages us to "become blameless and pure, 'children of God without fault in a warped and crooked generation.' Then you will shine among them like stars in the sky."

Living in the light is not an individual endeavor but a collective one. The church, as the body of Christ, is called to be a community of light, supporting and encouraging one another in faith. Hebrews 10:24-25 urges, "And let us consider how we may spur one another on toward love and good deeds, not giving up meeting together, as some are in the habit of doing, but encouraging one another—and all the more as you see the Day approaching."

As a community of light, we are to bear each other's burdens, pray for one another, and build each other up. 1 Thessalonians 5:11 instructs, "Therefore encourage one another and build each other up, just as in fact you are doing." Through fellowship and mutual support, we can grow in our faith and become more effective witnesses of Christ's light.

The impact of living in the light extends beyond our immediate surroundings. By faithfully reflecting God's light, we contribute to His eternal kingdom and leave a lasting legacy. Jesus assures us in Matthew 25:34-40 that our acts of service, no matter how small, are significant in His eyes and will be rewarded in eternity.

Moreover, living in the light brings us into closer communion with God. 1 John 1:7 promises, "But if we walk in the light, as he is in the light, we have fellowship with one another, and the blood of Jesus, his Son, purifies us from all sin." This fellowship with God and fellow believers enriches our spiritual journey and prepares us for the eternal light of His presence.

Living in the light is a continuous journey of transformation, guided by the truth of God's Word and empowered by His Spirit. As we strive to embody the light of Christ in our daily lives, we become reflections of His glory, illuminating the darkness around us and drawing others to His love.

May we embrace the call to be children of light, walking in integrity, reflecting Christ's love, engaging in good works, and overcoming darkness with good. Let us build a community of light, encouraging one another in faith and leaving an eternal impact for the glory of God.

As we live in the light, we anticipate the day when we will dwell in the eternal presence of God, where His glory will illuminate everything, and we will experience the fullness of His love and joy forever. Until then, let us shine brightly, living as beacons of hope in a world that desperately needs the light of Christ.

"To him who is able to keep you from stumbling and to present you before his glorious presence without fault and with great joy—to the only God our Savior be glory, majesty, power and authority, through Jesus Christ our Lord, before all ages, now and forevermore! Amen." (Jude 1:24-25)

CHAPTER 12

THE LIGHT OF CHRIST IN OUR DAILY LIVES

"In the same way, let your light shine before others, that they may see your good deeds and glorify your Father in heaven." - Matthew 5:16

In this concluding chapter, we delve into how the light of Christ permeates our daily lives, influencing our thoughts, actions, and interactions. The journey from darkness to light is not just a spiritual or abstract concept; it is a practical reality that should manifest in every aspect of our lives. We explore how to live out this light consistently, becoming effective witnesses of Christ's transformative power.

Living in the light of Christ means that our everyday actions should reflect His love and truth. It is about embodying the principles of the gospel in our daily routines. Colossians 3:17 instructs, "And whatever you do, whether in word or deed, do it all in the name of the Lord Jesus, giving thanks to God the Father through him." This means our work, conversations, and even mundane tasks should be done with a spirit of excellence and gratitude, reflecting the character of Christ.

Gratitude is a hallmark of living in the light. By cultivating a heart of gratitude, we acknowledge God's goodness and faithfulness in our lives. 1 Thessalonians 5:18 encourages us to "give thanks in all circumstances; for this is God's will for you in Christ Jesus." A grateful heart not only glorifies God but also transforms our perspective, helping us to see His light even in difficult situations.

The light of Christ should be evident in how we nurture our relationships. Jesus taught that love is the greatest commandment, and this love should be the foundation of our interactions with others. John 13:34-35 records Jesus saying, "A new command I give you: Love one another. As I have loved you, so you must love one another. By this, everyone will know that you are my disciples if you love one another."

Living in the light involves demonstrating love, patience, kindness, and forgiveness in our relationships. It means seeking reconciliation, supporting one another, and building each other up in faith.

Holiness is an integral part of living in the light. As children of God, we are called to be holy, just as He is holy (1 Peter 1:15-16). This involves making conscious choices to live according to God's standards, avoiding sinful behaviors, and striving for purity in our thoughts and actions.

Ephesians 4:22-24 advises, "You were taught, with regard to your former way of life, to put off your old self, which is being corrupted by its deceitful desires; to be made new in the attitude of your minds; and to put on the new self, created to be like God in true righteousness and holiness." Pursuing holiness means continually renewing our minds and aligning our lives with God's will.

Our light should extend beyond our personal lives to impact our communities. Jesus calls us to be the "light of the world" (Matthew 5:14), shining His truth and love in our neighborhoods, workplaces, and society at large. This involves actively engaging in our communities, serving others, and standing for justice and righteousness.

Isaiah 58:10 promises, "If you spend yourselves in behalf of the hungry and satisfy the needs of the oppressed, then your light will rise in the darkness, and your night will become like the noonday." By serving others and advocating for the marginalized, we become tangible expressions of God's light.

A vital aspect of living in the light is maintaining a consistent and fervent prayer life. Prayer connects us with God, strengthens our faith, and aligns our hearts with His purposes. Philippians 4:6-7 encourages us, "Do not be anxious about anything, but in every situation, by prayer and petition, with thanksgiving, present your requests to God. And the peace of God, which transcends all understanding, will guard your hearts and your minds in Christ Jesus."

Through prayer, we receive guidance, strength, and the assurance of God's presence, enabling us to live in the light even in challenging circumstances.

Living in the light also involves sharing the gospel with others. Jesus' Great Commission in Matthew 28:19-20 commands us to "go and make disciples of all nations, baptizing them in the name of the Father and of the Son and of the Holy Spirit, and teaching them to obey everything I have commanded you." Sharing our faith and witnessing to others about the transformative power of Christ's light is a crucial aspect of our spiritual journey.

Lastly, living in the light means having an eternal perspective. Colossians 3:1-2 exhorts us, "Since then, you have been raised with Christ, set your hearts on things above, where Christ is, seated at the right hand of God. Set your minds on things above, not on earthly things." By focusing on eternal truths and the hope of heaven, we are motivated to live faithfully and purposefully in this world.

The journey from darkness to light is a lifelong process of transformation, guided by the truth of God's Word and empowered by His Spirit. As we strive to live in the light of Christ, we reflect His glory, impact our world, and draw closer to Him. Our everyday actions, relationships, and choices become opportunities to shine His light, bringing hope and healing to those around us.

May we embrace this journey with faith, gratitude, love, holiness, service, prayer, evangelism, and an eternal perspective. As we live in the light, we not only experience the fullness of life in Christ but also pave the way for others to encounter His transformative power.

"And the city has no need of sun or moon, for the glory of God illuminates the city, and the Lamb is its light." (Revelation 21:23)

May the light of Christ shine brightly in and through us, leading us ever closer to the eternal glory of His presence. Amen.

CHAPTER 13

THEOLOGY OF LIGHT

"In him was life, and that life was the light of all mankind. The light shines in the darkness, and the darkness has not overcome it." - John 1:4-5

In this chapter, we explore the profound theological concept of light as it appears throughout Scripture. The metaphor of light serves as a powerful representation of God's presence, truth, holiness, and guidance. Understanding the theology of light deepens our comprehension of God's nature and His relationship with humanity.

From the very beginning, light is intrinsically connected to God's presence. In Genesis 1:3, God's first creative act is to say, "Let there be light," separating light from darkness. This act signifies God bringing order and clarity into chaos, highlighting His role as the source of life and order.

Light represents God's omnipresence and His divine revelation to humanity. In Exodus 13:21, we see God guiding the Israelites as a pillar of fire by night, providing them light and direction. This tangible manifestation of God's presence reassured His people of His continual guidance and protection.

Light in Scripture also symbolizes revelation and truth. The Psalmist declares, "Your word is a lamp for my feet, a light on my path" (Psalm 119:105), underscoring how God's Word illuminates the path of righteousness, guiding believers away from the darkness of ignorance and sin.

Jesus, as the incarnate Word, embodies this revelation. John 1:9 describes Jesus as "the true light that gives light to everyone," revealing God's nature and will to the world. His teachings and life provide a clear and truthful understanding of God, dispelling the darkness of falsehood and misunderstanding.

The purity and holiness of light are consistent themes throughout Scripture. Light is often used to illustrate God's absolute holiness and moral perfection. In 1 John 1:5, it is stated, "God is light; in him there is no darkness at all." This passage emphasizes God's unblemished purity and the absence of any sin or imperfection in Him.

Believers are called to reflect this holiness. Ephesians 5:8-9 instructs, "For you were once darkness, but now you are light in the Lord. Live as children of light (for the fruit of the light consists in all goodness, righteousness, and truth)." Our lives should reflect God's holy light, demonstrating goodness and righteousness in our conduct.

Light serves as a guide, leading believers in their spiritual journey. Proverbs 6:23 notes, "For this command is a lamp, this teaching is a light, and correction and instruction are the way to life." God's commandments provide guidance, helping us navigate life's complexities and make decisions that align with His will.

Jesus identifies Himself as the ultimate guide, saying in John 8:12, "I am the light of the world. Whoever follows me will never walk in darkness, but will have the light of life." By following Jesus, we receive divine direction and are led into a life of purpose and fulfillment.

Light is also a source of life, both physically and spiritually. Just as sunlight is essential for physical life, spiritual light is vital for our spiritual well-being. In John 1:4, we read, "In him was life, and that life was the light of all mankind." Jesus, as the light, imparts spiritual life and vitality, enabling us to live in communion with God.

This concept is further illustrated in Psalm 36:9, which states, "For with you is the fountain of life; in your light we see light." God's light illuminates our understanding, bringing spiritual enlightenment and growth.

The battle between light and darkness is a recurring theme in Scripture, symbolizing the struggle between good and evil, truth and falsehood. John 1:5 declares, "The light shines in the darkness, and the darkness has not overcome it." This verse reassures believers of the ultimate victory of light over darkness, emphasizing God's power and the inevitability of His triumph.

This struggle is evident in our daily lives as we contend with sin, temptation, and spiritual opposition. Ephesians 6:12 reminds us, "For our struggle is not against flesh and blood, but against the rulers, against the authorities, against the powers of this dark world and against the spiritual forces of evil in the heavenly realms." However, through God's light, we are empowered to overcome these challenges.

The gospel of Jesus Christ is often referred to as the light of the world. 2 Corinthians 4:4 highlights how "the god of this age has blinded the minds of unbelievers so that they cannot see the light of the gospel that displays the glory of Christ, who is the image of God." The gospel reveals the truth about God's redemptive plan and His love for humanity, bringing spiritual enlightenment to those who believe.

As recipients of this light, we are called to share it with others. Matthew 5:14-16 commissions us to be the light of the world, shining before others so they may see our good deeds and glorify our Father in heaven.

The ultimate fulfillment of the theology of light is found in the eternal state. Revelation 21:23 paints a picture of the New Jerusalem, where "the city does not need the sun or the moon to shine on it, for the glory of God gives it light, and the Lamb is its lamp." In eternity, God's presence will be the source of all light, dispelling all darkness and illuminating His eternal kingdom.

This vision offers believers hope and assurance of a future where they will dwell in the perpetual light of God's presence, free from sin, sorrow, and suffering.

The theology of light encompasses a rich tapestry of themes that reveal the nature of God and His relationship with humanity. Light represents God's presence, truth, holiness, guidance, life, and victory over darkness. As believers, we are called to live in this light, reflecting it in our daily lives and sharing it with the world.

May we continually seek to walk in the light, allowing God's truth to guide us, His holiness to purify us, and His presence to illuminate our paths. As we do so, we become beacons of His love and truth, drawing others to the eternal light of Christ.

"And the city has no need of sun or moon, for the glory of God illuminates the city, and the Lamb is its light." (Revelation 21:23)

Let us live as children of light, shining brightly in a world that desperately needs the hope and life that only Christ can offer. Amen.

CHAPTER 14

THEOLOGY OF DARKNESS

"This is the verdict: Light has come into the world, but people loved darkness instead of light because their deeds were evil." - John 3:19

In this chapter, we explore the theological concept of darkness as it appears throughout Scripture. Darkness serves as a profound metaphor for evil, sin, ignorance, and separation from God. Understanding the theology of darkness deepens our awareness of the gravity of sin and the transformative power of God's light.

Throughout the Bible, darkness is often associated with evil and sin. It represents the antithesis of God's holiness and purity. In Ephesians 5:11, Paul admonishes believers, "Have nothing to do with the fruitless deeds of darkness, but rather expose them." This verse underscores the inherent unfruitfulness and destructiveness of sinful behaviors.

The fall of humanity introduced darkness into the world. Genesis 3 recounts how Adam and Eve's disobedience brought sin and spiritual darkness, corrupting God's perfect creation. This original sin plunged humanity into a state of moral and spiritual darkness, necessitating redemption.

Darkness also symbolizes separation from God, the source of all light and life. In Isaiah 59:2, we read, "But your iniquities have separated you from your God; your sins have hidden his face from you so that he will not hear." Sin creates a barrier between humanity and God, plunging individuals into spiritual darkness and alienation.

This separation is poignantly illustrated in Jesus' crucifixion. As Jesus bore the sins of the world, darkness covered the land for three hours (Matthew 27:45). This darkness symbolized the profound separation Jesus experienced from the Father as He took on the sins of humanity.

Darkness in Scripture often denotes ignorance and deception. In John 12:35, Jesus warns, "You are going to have the light just a little while longer. Walk while you have the light before darkness overtakes you. Whoever walks in the dark does not know where they are going." This verse highlights the disorientation and confusion that come from spiritual ignorance and the absence of divine truth.

Satan, the "prince of darkness," is described as the deceiver who blinds the minds of unbelievers to keep them in spiritual darkness (2 Corinthians 4:4). His lies and deceptions keep people from understanding and accepting the truth of the gospel, leading them further away from God.

The power of darkness is evident in the spiritual battles that believers face. Ephesians 6:12 states, "For our struggle is not against flesh and blood, but against the rulers, against the authorities, against the powers of this dark world and against the spiritual forces of evil in the heavenly realms." This verse reveals that darkness encompasses not just sin and ignorance but also spiritual forces that oppose God and His purposes.

The power of darkness is pervasive and insidious, seeking to undermine and destroy the faith of believers. Yet, the Bible assures us that God's power is greater and that through Christ, we can overcome the forces of darkness.

Living in darkness has dire consequences. It leads to spiritual death, separation from God, and eternal condemnation. Romans 6:23 declares, "For the wages of sin is death, but the gift of God is eternal life in Christ Jesus our Lord." Sin and darkness result in death, both physical and spiritual, underscoring the seriousness of living apart from God's light.

Jesus describes hell as a place of "outer darkness" where there is "weeping and gnashing of teeth" (Matthew 8:12). This depiction highlights the eternal consequences of rejecting God's light and remaining in spiritual darkness.

The good news of the gospel is that God has provided a way for us to be delivered from darkness. Colossians 1:13 proclaims, "For he has rescued us from the dominion of darkness and brought us into the kingdom of the Son he loves." Through Jesus Christ, we are redeemed from the power of darkness and transferred into His glorious light.

This deliverance is made possible by Jesus' sacrificial death and resurrection. In John 12:46, Jesus declares, "I have come into the world as a light so that no one who believes in me should stay in darkness." By believing in Jesus, we receive the light of life and are liberated from the bondage of sin and darkness.

Believers are called to leave the darkness and walk in the light. 1 Peter 2:9 describes our new identity in Christ: "But you are a chosen people, a royal priesthood, a holy nation, God's special possession, that you may declare the praises of him who called you out of darkness into his wonderful light."

This verse emphasizes our calling to live distinct and holy lives, reflecting God's light to the world.

Leaving darkness involves repentance, turning away from sin, and embracing God's truth. Ephesians 5:8-9 encourages us, "For you were once darkness, but now you are light in the Lord. Live as children of light (for the fruit of the light consists in all goodness, righteousness, and truth)."

Ultimately, victory over darkness is assured through Christ. John 1:5 confidently states, "The light shines in the darkness, and the darkness has not overcome it." This assurance is rooted in Jesus' triumph over sin, death, and Satan through His resurrection.

Believers are called to live in this victory, empowered by the Holy Spirit to overcome the darkness in their own lives and in the world. Romans 13:12 exhorts us, "The night is nearly over; the day is almost here. So let us put aside the deeds of darkness and put on the armor of light."

The theology of darkness reveals the stark reality of sin, separation, and spiritual opposition that humanity faces. It underscores the need for God's redemptive light to penetrate and overcome this darkness. Through Jesus Christ, we are offered deliverance, restoration, and the assurance of eternal life in God's glorious light.

As we navigate our spiritual journey, let us remain vigilant against the forces of darkness, steadfast in our faith, and committed to living as children of light. By doing so, we not only experience the fullness of life in Christ but also shine His transformative light into a world desperately in need of hope and redemption.

"The light shines in the darkness, and the darkness has not overcome it." (John 1:5)

May we walk confidently in the light of Christ, bearing witness to His victory and illuminating the path for others to follow? Amen.

CHAPTER 15

LIVING AS CHILDREN OF LIGHT

"For you were once darkness, but now you are light in the Lord. Live as children of light." - Ephesians 5:8

As we conclude this theological journey from darkness to light, we turn our focus to living out our new identity as children of light. This chapter explores the practical implications of our transformation and the call to reflect God's light in every aspect of our lives. It delves into how we can embody the light of Christ, impacting our world and drawing others to Him.

Our journey begins with embracing our new identity in Christ. Ephesians 5:8 reminds us that we were once darkness, but now we are light in the Lord. This fundamental change calls us to live differently, reflecting the light of Christ in our thoughts, words, and actions.

This new identity is not merely a title but a reality that transforms us from within. 2 Corinthians 5:17 declares, "Therefore, if anyone is in Christ, the new creation has come: The old has gone, the new is here!" We are called to leave behind our old ways of living in darkness and fully embrace our new life in the light.

Living as children of light means reflecting God's character in our daily lives. This involves embodying the virtues of goodness, righteousness, and truth. Ephesians 5:9 states, "For the fruit of the light consists in all goodness, righteousness, and truth."

Goodness involves actively doing what is right and beneficial for others. It requires kindness, compassion, and a genuine concern for the well-being of those around us. Righteousness means living in a way that aligns with God's standards and commands. It calls for integrity, honesty, and moral uprightness. Truth entails living transparently and authentically, without deceit or hypocrisy.

One of the most profound ways to live as children of light is by walking in love. 1 John 4:7-8 encourages us, "Dear friends, let us love one another, for love comes from God. Everyone who loves has been born of God and knows God. Whoever does not love does not know God, because God is love."

Love is the essence of God's nature and should be the hallmark of our lives as His children. This love is sacrificial, selfless, and unconditional, mirroring the love that Christ demonstrated on the cross. By loving others, we reflect the light of God's love and draw them closer to Him.

As children of light, we are called to bear witness to the light of Christ. Matthew 5:14-16 charges us, "You are the light of the world. A town built on a hill cannot be hidden. Neither do people light a lamp and put it under a bowl. Instead, they put it on its stand, and it gives light to everyone in the house. In the same way, let your light shine before others, that they may see your good deeds and glorify your Father in heaven."

Our lives should be a testimony to the transformative power of God's light. This involves sharing the gospel, living out our faith authentically, and being a positive influence in our communities. Our good deeds should point others to Christ, bringing glory to God and expanding His kingdom.

Living as children of light often means shining in a dark world. Philippians 2:15-16 exhorts us, "So that you may become blameless and pure, children of God without fault in a warped and crooked generation. Then you will shine among them like stars in the sky as you hold firmly to the word of life."

The world is filled with darkness—sin, suffering, and spiritual blindness. As followers of Christ, we are called to be beacons of hope and truth, illuminating the way for others. This requires courage, resilience, and unwavering faith, as we face opposition and challenges.

Overcoming darkness is an ongoing process that involves continual reliance on God's strength and guidance. Ephesians 6:10-11 instructs us, "Finally, be strong in the Lord and in his mighty power. Put on the full armor of God, so that you can take your stand against the devil's schemes."

The full armor of God includes truth, righteousness, the gospel of peace, faith, salvation, and the word of God. These spiritual tools equip us to withstand the attacks of darkness and stand firm in our faith. Prayer and dependence on the Holy Spirit are essential in this battle, as we seek God's wisdom and strength.

Cultivating a life of light requires intentional spiritual practices that draw us closer to God and deepen our faith. Regular engagement with Scripture, prayer, worship, and fellowship with other believers are vital components of a vibrant spiritual life.

Psalm 119:105 reminds us, "Your word is a lamp for my feet, a light on my path." Immersing ourselves in God's Word illuminates our understanding and guides our steps.

Prayer fosters intimacy with God, allowing us to align our hearts with His will. Worship and fellowship provide encouragement and accountability, strengthening our resolve to live as children of light.

Ultimately, living as children of light means fulfilling the unique calling that God has placed on each of our lives. Ephesians 2:10 declares, "For we are God's handiwork, created in Christ Jesus to do good works, which God prepared in advance for us to do."

God has a specific purpose and plan for each of us, and living in the light involves discovering and pursuing that calling. Whether it is through our vocations, relationships, ministries, or acts of service, we are called to glorify God and make a positive impact in the world.

Our journey from darkness to light is a transformative and ongoing process. As children of light, we are called to reflect God's character, walk in love, bear witness to Christ, shine in a dark world, overcome darkness, and cultivate a life of light. By embracing our new identity in Christ and living out our calling, we become beacons of hope and truth in a world desperately in need of God's light.

"For you were once darkness, but now you are light in the Lord. Live as children of light." (Ephesians 5:8)

May we continually seek to live in the light, drawing closer to God and reflecting His glory in every aspect of our lives. As we do so, we bring honor to His name and lead others into the transformative power of His light. Amen.